WORDPRESS WIZARDRY

A Beginner's Guide to Building Your Online Presence

Ashley J. Collins

Introduction

What is WordPress?

Why Use WordPress?

Getting Started with WordPress

Chapter 1: Setting Up Your WordPress Site

Choosing a Domain Name

Selecting a Hosting Provider

Installing WordPress

Configuring Basic Settings

Chapter 2: Understanding the WordPress Dashboard

Navigating the Dashboard

Customizing the Dashboard Creating Content

Writing and Formatting Posts

Adding Media (Images, Videos)

Managing Categories and Tags

Chapter 3: Customizing Your WordPress Site

Choosing and Installing Themes

Customizing Themes

Using Widgets and Menus

Chapter 4: Essential Plugins

Introduction to Plugins

Installing and Activating Plugins

Must-Have Plugins for Beginners

Chapter 5: Managing Users and Comments

User Roles and Permissions

Dealing with Comments

Chapter 6 SEO Basics for WordPress

Understanding SEO

Using SEO Plugins
Chapter 7: Security Best Practices
Securing Your WordPress Site
Regular Backups
Updates and Maintenance
Chapter 8: Troubleshooting Common Issues
Diagnosing and Fixing Problems
Chapter 9: Growing Your WordPress Skills
Further Learning Resources
Joining WordPress Communities
Exploring Advanced Features
Chapter 10: Conclusion
Recap and Next Steps
Embracing Your WordPress Journey

Introduction

What is WordPress?

WordPress is a famous substance of the executive's framework (CMS) that permits clients to effectively make and oversee sites. It offers a scope of subjects, modules, and customization choices, making it flexible for different web projects.

WordPress began as publishing content to a blog stage yet has developed into an adaptable CMS utilized for different sites, including web journals, business destinations, and internet business. Its easy-to-use interface requires no coding skill, empowering individuals to productively distribute and oversee online substance.

WordPress is an open-source stage, cultivating an immense local area of designers who contribute topics and modules. Its broad module biological system permits clients to add highlights and usefulness to their destinations, fitting them to explicit necessities. Moreover, customary updates improve security and execution.

WordPress works on a PHP and MySQL system, giving a dynamic and intuitive site insight. Its adaptable nature makes it reasonable for novices and high-level clients the same, supporting different media types and responsive plans for ideal review on various gadgets.

Outstandingly, WordPress upholds Website design enhancement works, supporting better permeability on web crawlers. With plenty of accessible subjects and the capacity to make handicrafts, clients can accomplish a novel search for their sites. Its fame likewise implies an abundance of online assets, instructional exercises, and discussions for help and investigation.

WordPress' value lies in its availability and flexibility. It enables clients, even those without broad specialized information, to easily make and oversee sites. Whether for web journals, business locales, or internet business, its flexibility and rich biological system make it an amazing asset for different web-based tries.

Past convenience, WordPress works with cooperation with its multi-client ability, permitting groups to cooperatively contribute and oversee content. Its versatility obliges development, making it reasonable for little online journals or enormous-scope corporate sites. The stage's ordinary updates and dynamic local area support guarantee continuous enhancements and help.

Additionally, WordPress gives strong investigation apparatuses, empowering clients to follow site execution and guest conduct. Its coordination with different outsider administrations improves usefulness, from virtual entertainment sharing to online business exchanges. The stage's worldwide reach and broad reception highlight its unwavering quality and viability in the steadily advancing scene of web advancement.

Why Use WordPress?

WordPress is famous for its easy-to-use interface, broad module environment, and vigorous local area support. It's flexible, making it appropriate for different sites, from online journals to internet business. Furthermore, its open-source nature takes into consideration customization, and standard updates improve security and usefulness.

WordPress offers many subjects and modules, permitting clients to effectively redo the plan and add highlights without broad coding. Its substance the executive's framework (CMS) works on distributing, and Web optimization agreeable instruments assist with further developing web index rankings. The enormous local area implies plentiful assets, instructional exercises, and investigating help. Generally, it's an adaptable and versatile stage for people and organizations the same.

Besides, WordPress works with coordinated effort with numerous clients and gives job-based admittance control. It's continually developing, adjusting to industry patterns, and supports sight and sound substance flawlessly. The stage's responsive plan guarantees similarity with different gadgets, adding to a positive client experience. Whether you're a novice or an accomplished designer, WordPress stays a flexible and strong decision for site creation.

Critically, WordPress appreciates far-reaching reception, making it simple to track down engineers, fashioners, and different experts acquainted with the stage. This can lessen expenses and increase the availability of skills. Its broad documentation and local area gatherings further upgrade the expectation to learn and adapt for clients of all expertise levels, encouraging a strong climate for that structure and keeping up with sites.

Moreover, WordPress brags an enormous environment of outsider instruments and mixes, smoothing out errands like examination, email showcasing, and virtual entertainment on the board. Its obligation to openness and inclusivity guarantees that sites made on the stage can contact a different crowd. With customary updates and a guarantee of security, WordPress remains a dependable decision for those looking for a stable and component-rich site arrangement.

Furthermore, WordPress' adaptability is vital; it obliges the development of sites, whether they begin little and extend once again time. The stage's multilingual help makes it a worldwide answer for sites taking care of different crowds. Its inherent contribution to a blog's capacities likewise makes it a great decision for individuals who focus on happy creation and regular updates. Generally speaking, WordPress offers a far-reaching bundle that lines up with the developing requirements of site proprietors.

WordPress focuses on portable responsiveness, guaranteeing that sites look and capability well on cell phones and tablets. This is essential given the rising commonness of portable clients. The stage's natural dashboard works on the location of the board, permitting clients to refresh content, screen examination, and make changes without any problem. With a solid accentuation on local area input, WordPress keeps on refining its elements, preparing it as a dynamic and future decision for different web-based projects.

Getting Started with WordPress

To begin with WordPress, first, pick a facilitating supplier like Bluehost or SiteGround. Introduce WordPress through your facilitating account, then, at that point, pick a subject and redo it. Investigate modules for added usefulness, and make your most memorable pages and posts. Get to know the dashboard and settings to deal with your site.

Investigate the WordPress dashboard to redo your site's appearance, add fundamental modules for Website design enhancement and security, and set up classes and labels for coordinated content. Routinely update subjects, modules, and WordPress itself to guarantee security and ideal execution. Use instructional exercises and discussions to investigate and extend your WordPress abilities.

Consider making a steady posting plan for your substance and influence online entertainment to advance your website. Investigate WordPress Website design enhancement best practices to work on your web page's perceivability in web crawlers. Draw in with your crowd through remarks and energize client connection. Reinforcement your site consistently and remain informed about the most recent WordPress updates and patterns.

Use WordPress investigation apparatuses to follow site execution, client conduct, and famous substance. Investigate internet business choices assuming that you intend to sell items. Find out about fundamental HTML and CSS for further developed customization. Join the WordPress people group and go to meetups or online classes to associate with different clients and remain refreshed on industry patterns.

Execute a portable responsive plan to take care of clients on various gadgets. Enhance your pictures for quicker stacking times. Make a convincing "About" page and remember a reasonable source of inspiration for your landing page. Use highlighted pictures for visual allure in your posts. Consider carrying out a contact structure to work with correspondence with your crowd. Routinely survey and update your site's substance to keep it new and significant.

Jump into cutting-edge highlights like custom post types and scientific categorizations for particular substance associations. Find out about the significance of permalinks and set them up for site design improvement. Find out about WordPress safety efforts, like solid passwords and two-factor confirmation. Investigate ways of further developing site speed, such as reserving modules. Consider executing a reinforcement system, including both computerized and manual reinforcements.

Investigate the universe of WordPress youngster subjects for more secure topic customization without influencing the fundamental topic. Find out about the Gutenberg block proofreader for more adaptable substance creation. Consider carrying out a substance conveyance organization (CDN) to streamline stacking times internationally. Find out about WordPress multisite on the off chance that you intend to deal with numerous locales from one establishment. Try different things with A/B testing to enhance your site's components for better client commitment and change rates.

Chapter 1: Setting Up Your WordPress Site

Choosing a Domain Name

Select a space that mirrors your site's motivation, is not difficult to recall, and is ideally short. Consider utilizing catchphrases connected with your substance and guaranteeing it's one of a kind. Check for space accessibility and go for the gold expansion like .com.

Stay away from dashes, numbers, or complex spellings to improve client review. Guarantee it's pertinent to your image or content, making it simpler for guests to connect with your site. Moreover, look at web-based entertainment accessibility for consistency across stages.

Focus on clearness over intelligence, it is effectively spelled and articulated to guarantee your space. Research contenders' spaces to stick out and pick an immortal name that will not immediately become obsolete. Consider the drawn-out brand picture and potential for development. Finally, twofold check for any brand name clashes.

Remember the worldwide crowd by keeping away from locale-explicit terms except if your substance focuses on a particular area. Use area name generators for motivation and to investigate varieties. Test likely names with companions or associates to assemble input on memorability and clearness. Finally, register your picked area expeditiously to get it.

Check for space accessibility on well-known enlistment centers and secure it for a drawn-out period to stay away from lapse issues. Go for the gold that lines up with your substance technique, making a firm web-based presence. Guarantee the area doesn't restrict your tentative arrangements for the site's development or venture into various points.

Consider the simplicity of verbal correspondence while sharing your space - it ought to be easily passed on via telephone or face-to-face. Try not to utilize protected terms or incorrect spellings to forestall legitimate intricacies. Finally, ponder how your space will thoroughly search in composed structure, as a clean and outwardly engaging name can have an enduring effect on guests.

Lead a space name search to affirm there are no bad affiliations or history attached to your picked name. Research expected varieties to stay away from accidental associations with irrelevant substances or brands. Moreover, contemplate the potential for Website design enhancement advancement by integrating important catchphrases into your area, if material to your substance methodology.

Guarantee your picked space abuses no industry-explicit guidelines, particularly assuming your site covers touchy subjects. Confirm the space's set of experiences to try not to acquire any punishments or issues from a past proprietor. Finally, contemplate versatility - pick a space that can oblige future changes or extensions in your site's concentration or contributions.

Consider client trust by choosing a safe HTTPS convention for your space. Assess the conceivability of your area when stood up clearly, limiting the opportunity of mistaken assumptions. Use devices to check for normal incorrect spellings to keep away from possible disarray for guests. At long last, adjust your space to your marking system to make a firm internet-based character.

Selecting a Hosting Provider

Consider trustworthy facilitating suppliers like Bluehost, SiteGround, or Kinsta for WordPress. Assess in light of execution, backing, security, and estimating to track down the best met for your requirements.

Think about highlights like programmed reinforcements, SSL authentications, and versatility. Peruse client audits to check consumer loyalty. Additionally, check for the simplicity of WordPress establishment and solid client service.

Investigate server execution and speed, as quicker stacking times are vital for client experience and Website design enhancement. Consider the facilitating supplier's server farm areas to guarantee vicinity to your interest group for upgraded speed. Furthermore, evaluate any extra administrations or apparatuses they offer for WordPress advancement and security.

Look at the facilitating supplier's update choices for future versatility. Guarantee they give an easy-to-understand control board for simple site the executives. Look at the terms of administration, particularly with respect as far as possible, uptime ensures, and any expected limitations. Finally, ask about their relocation support on the off chance that you're moving a current WordPress site.

Investigate the facilitating supplier's client assistance channels and responsiveness. Search for all-day, everyday support through live visits, email, or telephone. Consider their insight base and local area gatherings for self-improvement assets. Focus on the facilitating supplier's standing for dealing with security issues and their obligation to customary updates and fixes.

Assess the estimating structure and think about long-haul costs. A few suppliers might offer early rates that increment upon restoration. Check for any secret expenses and evaluate assuming the facilitating plan lines up with your site's current and future necessities. Moreover, affirm the supplier's discount strategy if you want to make changes or switch facilitating administrations.

Research the reinforcement choices given by the facilitating supplier and whether they offer robotized reinforcements. Comprehend the reclamation cycle in the event of information misfortune. It's fundamental to have a solid reinforcement framework to protect your WordPress site. Moreover, check if the facilitating plan incorporates a substance conveyance organization (CDN) for further developed site execution and quicker stacking times worldwide.

Consider the facilitating supplier's position on supportability and ecological obligation, as this could line up with your qualities. A few suppliers focus on green facilitating rehearses. Additionally, observe the terms for scaling assets, for example, redesigning RAM or capacity, to oblige your site's development. Finally, investigate any additional items or highlights offered, like arranging conditions, reserving choices, or single-tick establishments for WordPress modules.

Installing WordPress

To introduce WordPress, you regularly need a web have. Here is an overall outline of introducing WordPress:

Pick a Space and Facilitate:

Select a space name for your site.

Pick a solid web-facilitating supplier.

Introduce WordPress:

Many facilitating suppliers offer a single-tick WordPress establishment. Check your facilitating dashboard for choices like "Softaculous" or "Installatron."

Manual Establishment (if necessary):

Download the most recent WordPress rendition from the authority site.

Transfer the documents to your web server utilizing FTP.

Make an Information base:

Most facilitating suppliers likewise permit you to make an information base through their dashboards.

Observe the data set name, username, and secret phrase.

Arrange wp-config.php:

Find the wp-config-sample.php document in your WordPress records.

Rename it to wp-config.php and alter it.

Enter your data set data.

Run the Establishment:

Visit your space in an internet browser.

Complete the WordPress arrangement by entering site subtleties, usernames, and secret keys.

Login to Your Dashboard:

Access your WordPress administrator dashboard utilizing the login qualifications you recently set.

That is an essential outline; the specific advances can change in light of your facilitating supplier.

The following are a couple of extra tips for your WordPress arrangement:

Pick a Subject:

Investigate and choose a subject for your web composition. You can find free and premium topics in the WordPress subject registry or from outsider suppliers.

Introduce Fundamental Modules:

Add usefulness to your site by introducing modules. Well-known ones incorporate Yoast Website design enhancement for site improvement, Akismet for spam insurance, and Contact Structure 7 for making structures.

Modify Permalinks:

Set up Website optimization agreeable permalinks under Settings > Permalinks. Pick a construction that mirrors your substance-ordered progression.

Make Fundamental Pages:

Create fundamental pages like Home, About Us, Contact, and Security Strategy. You can do this from the WordPress dashboard under Pages > Add New.

Design Understanding Settings:

Characterize the first page and posts page under Settings > Perusing. Pick whether you need your most recent posts or a static page as the first page.

Set Up Classifications and Labels:

Coordinate your substance by making classifications and labels. This further develops routes and assists web search tools with grasping your website's design.

Streamline Media Settings:

Change the picture sizes under Settings > Media to guarantee pictures are fittingly measured for your subject and don't dial back your site.

Standard Reinforcements:

Execute a reinforcement arrangement. Many facilitating suppliers offer programmed reinforcements, or you can utilize modules like UpdraftPlus.

Keep WordPress Refreshed:

Consistently update WordPress, subjects, and modules to profit from security fixes and new elements.

Investigate Extra Settings:

Find out about settings connected with conversation, remarks, and client jobs to redo your site as per your inclinations.

The following are a couple of additional ways to streamline your WordPress site:

Execution Improvement:

Utilize a reserving module like W3 All out Store or WP Super Store to further develop page load times.

Streamline pictures before transferring them. Modules like Smush or EWWW Picture Analyzer can help.

Safety efforts:

Introduce a security module like Wordfence or Sucuri to shield your site from noxious exercises.

Utilize solid, one-of-a-kind passwords for your WordPress login and data set.

Versatile Responsiveness:

Guarantee your picked topic is versatile. A responsive plan is pivotal for giving a decent client experience on different gadgets.

Online Entertainment Coordination:

Interface your site to your web-based entertainment accounts. Many subjects accompany worked in web-based entertainment choices, or you can utilize modules for this reason.

Google Examination Reconciliation:

Set up Google Examination to follow your site's exhibition and guest conduct. You can utilize modules like MonsterInsights for simple joining.

Alter Gadgets:

Use gadgets to add usefulness to your sidebar or other widgetized regions on your site. Well-known gadgets incorporate late posts, classifications, and web-based entertainment takes care of.

SSL Testament:

Empower HTTPS on your site by introducing an SSL testament. Many facilitating suppliers offer free SSL testaments through We Should Scramble.

Survey and Moderate Remarks:

Consistently check and moderate remarks on your site. Answer client commitment and channel out spam.

Make a Favicon:

Transfer a custom favicon under Appearance > Modify. This little symbol shows up in program tabs and bookmarks, improving your site's marking.

Test Your Site:

Consistently test your site's usefulness, particularly after making changes. Guarantee it functions admirably across various programs and gadgets.

Keep in mind, that progressing upkeep is pivotal for a sound WordPress site.

Configuring Basic Settings

To design fundamental settings in WordPress, sign in to your administrator dashboard. Explore "Settings" in the left menu. Change general settings like site title, slogan, and URL in the "General" tab. Set your favored time region and date design. Save changes to apply.

Investigate the "Permalinks" segment to alter your URL structure. In "Perusing," set landing page and post-show inclinations. "Conversation" oversees remark settings. "Media" controls transfer settings. Survey "Protection" for site perceivability choices. Save changes after changes.

Check the "Expressing" settings to design default post classifications, post-design inclinations, and the composing connection point. "Perusing" permits you to set a static first page and control the number of blog entries shown. The "Conversation" tab allows you to oversee remark settings, while "Media" characterizes picture sizes. Finally, "Security" gives choices to web crawler perceivability. Change and save settings on a case-by-case basis.

Investigate the "Permalinks" segment to redo URL structures for posts and pages. "Overall," set your site's title, slogan, and URL. "Stating" permits default post classes and arrangement inclinations. "Perusing" allows you to pick a static first page and control post-show. Oversee remarks in the

"Conversation" tab. "Media" controls transfer settings. Finally, check "Security" for web crawler permeability. Save changes to apply arrangements.

For extra customization, think about introducing subjects and modules. Subjects control your site's appearance, while modules add usefulness. Access "Appearance" to introduce or modify subjects. In "Modules," you can add new ones and oversee existing ones. Consistently update WordPress, subjects, and modules to guarantee security and ideal execution. Investigate the "Clients" segment to oversee client jobs and consents. Reinforcement your site routinely to forestall information misfortune.

To upgrade security, change the default "administrator" username and utilize areas of strength for a. Use the "Instruments" segment for bringing in/trading content. Introduce a storing module for further developed site speed. Consistently screen and moderate remarks to keep a sound conversation climate. Investigate the "Gadgets" segment to redo your site's sidebar and other widgetized regions. Dive more deeply into the block manager for effective substance creation. Consistently survey and update your site's substance for significance.

Consider executing Website optimization rehearses by utilizing a Search engine optimization module to upgrade your webpage for web indexes. Design your site's route menu under "Appearance" for an easy-to-use insight. Make a custom 404 mistake page to direct guests when a page isn't found. Set up Google Investigation for point-by-point site examination. Routinely check for broken joins utilizing modules or online devices. Use the "Customizer" for ongoing sneak peeks of topic changes. Watch out for site execution and improve pictures for quicker stacking times.

Wordpress

Chapter 2: Understanding the WordPress Dashboard

Navigating the Dashboard

To explore the WordPress dashboard, utilize the left-hand menu for different areas like Posts, Pages, Media, and Appearance. Tweak your site, add content, and oversee settings from that point.

Investigate the "Posts" segment to make and oversee blog entries, "Pages" for static substance, and "Media" for transferring and overseeing records. "Appearance" allows you to redo subjects, gadgets, and menus. "Settings" permits design, for example, site title and permalink structure.

In the "Posts" area, you can order and label your articles. Use the "Pages" area for fundamental site pages like About Us or Contact. The "Media" library stores pictures and documents, while "Appearance" allows you to change subjects or add new ones. "Settings" covers general designs for your site.

For a powerful site, think about utilizing "Modules" to add usefulness. Screen remarks under "Remarks," and break down site details with "Dashboard" or a device like Google Investigation. Find out more about these areas for far-reaching WordPress executives.

The "Clients" area permits you to oversee client jobs and authorizations. "Apparatuses" frequently incorporate choices for bringing in/sending out happiness. Consistently check for refreshes in the "Updates" segment to guarantee your WordPress establishment and modules are current for security and execution.

The "Customizer" under "Appearance" is convenient for live seeing topic changes. "Gadgets" allows you to add content to explicit regions of your site, similar to sidebars. Investigate these elements to fit your site's appearance and usefulness as per your inclinations.

Consider investigating the "Gutenberg" block manager for instinctive substance creation. It permits you to structure happy with blocks, making it more straightforward to plan and organize your pages and posts. Explore different avenues regarding these apparatuses to improve your by and large WordPress experience.

In the "Gutenberg" manager, influence highlights like reusable blocks for proficiency. Also, use the "Classes" and "Labels" choices in the "Posts" segment to arrange your substance. These systems can smooth out satisfied creation and upgrade site routes.

Inside the "Gutenberg" proofreader, explore different avenues regarding block examples to effortlessly add predefined designs. Investigate the "Custom Fields" in the "Page" and "Post" editors for cutting-edge content customization. These highlights offer adaptability and imagination in creating your site content.

For cutting-edge clients, diving into the "Topic Supervisor" permits direct code alteration for exact customization. In any case, practice watchfulness and back up your site before making changes to stay away from possible issues. This can be especially helpful for adjusting your WordPress subject to match explicit prerequisites.

To upgrade Website design enhancement, utilize the "Yoast Web optimization" module for streamlining content and working on your web page's perceivability on web search tools. Routinely back up your site utilizing modules like "UpdraftPlus" for added security. These practices add to a very much kept up with and enhanced WordPress site.

Consider investigating the "Elementor" module for intuitive page building, giving a visual method for planning and tweaking your site. This can be particularly valuable for clients looking for an additional way to deal with making and changing their WordPress pages.

Customizing the Dashboard Creating Content

To alter your WordPress dashboard, you can utilize modules like "Administrator Segments" or "Custom Dashboard Gadgets." For making content, explore the "Posts" or "Pages" area in the administrator board, then click "Add New." Modify your substance utilizing the proofreader and media choices accessible.

To additionally modify your WordPress dashboard, consider changing the design with modules, for example, "Adminimize" or "Extreme Dashboard." For content creation, investigate the Gutenberg proofreader for a block-based approach, permitting you to add different components to your posts or pages without any problem. Moreover, investigate subjects and topic choices for a firm visual plan.

To improve content creation in WordPress, investigate modules like "Yoast Search engine optimization" for streamlining your posts, and "Elementor" for cutting-edge pages working with a simplified connection point. Use classes and labels to arrange content actually, and routinely update modules and subjects to guarantee security and execution. Consider incorporating online entertainment-sharing choices to advance your substance across stages.

For a consistent client experience, enhance pictures before transferring to further develop site speed. Use the "Highlighted Picture" choice to upgrade visual allure in post postings. Carry out a remark control framework to draw in with your crowd. Consistently reinforce your site utilizing modules like "UpdraftPlus" for security and true serenity. Finally, investigate examination apparatuses, for example, Google Examination for bits of knowledge into client conduct and traffic sources.

Consider making a custom menu through the "Appearance" > "Menus" segment to control the route structure. Carry out a reserving module like "W3 Complete Store" to support page stacking times. Investigate "Custom Post Types" and "Scientific classifications" for more particular substance associations. For cutting-edge clients, dive into the functions.php record in your subject for extra customizations and changes. Continuously make sure to keep your WordPress establishment, modules, and subjects refreshed for security and execution enhancements.

To improve client commitment, empower client enlistment, and use modules like "BuddyPress" for making a local area inside your WordPress site. Try different things with A/B testing utilizing instruments like "Optimizely" to enhance your substance and design given client inclinations. Investigate internet business abilities by incorporating modules like "WooCommerce" for selling items or administrations straightforwardly from your website. Routinely survey and enhance your site's Website optimization system to further develop perceivability in web search tool results.

Investigate availability modules like "WP Openness" to guarantee your webpage is comprehensive and follows web openness principles. Execute a responsive plan or a versatile subject to improve the client experience on different gadgets. Use the "Customizer" for constant seeing of topic changes before applying them. Consider setting up an organizing climate to test significant changes before sending them to your live site. In conclusion, draw in with the WordPress people group through discussions and instructional exercises for progressing learning and backing.

To cultivate peruser cooperation, energize remarks on your posts, and answer quickly. Influence email showcasing by incorporating devices like "Mailchimp" to fabricate a supporter base and send bulletins. Use the "Jetpack" module for extra elements like site details, social sharing, and margin time checking. Routinely review and upgrade your site's exhibition utilizing instruments like "GTmetrix" or "Pingdom" to guarantee quick stacking times. Furthermore, come up with a strong reinforcement methodology involving both on-location and off-site reinforcements for added security.

To improve security, utilize areas of strength for a strategy and consider utilizing a security module like "Sucuri" or "Wordfence." Carry out SSL for a protected association, particularly if dealing with delicate data. Screen client action with instruments like "Action Log" modules to remain informed about changes on your site. Consistently review and tidy up your media library and information base to enhance capacity and further develop site execution. Ultimately, remain informed about WordPress refreshes, industry patterns, and best practices for progressing site the board and improvement.

Consider executing a substance conveyance organization (CDN) to disperse your site's resources across servers universally, further developing stacking times for guests from different areas. Investigate blueprint markup to upgrade your site's web search tool permeability and give more extravagant bits in list items. Use the "WP-Enhance" module to routinely tidy up and advance your data set. On the off chance that material, investigate multilingual modules like "WPML" to contact a more extensive crowd. Consistently survey and refine your site's route and client stream for a consistent encounter.

Try different things with organized information and rich scraps utilizing Schema.org markup to improve how web crawlers comprehend and show your substance. Use storing systems, for example, program reserving and object reserving for ideal execution. Execute apathetic stacking for pictures to further develop page stacking times. Investigate the combination of Google Examination for inside and out bits of knowledge into client conduct and site execution. Finally, lead ordinary site reviews to recognize and fix any messed up joins, guaranteeing a smooth perusing experience for your guests.

Writing and Formatting Posts

To compose and organize posts in WordPress:

Log in to WordPress:

Access your WordPress dashboard.

Make Another Post:

Explore to "Posts" and snap "Add New."

Compose Content:

Enter your post's title in the given field.

Add your substance to the principal manager.

Text Designing:

Utilize the toolbar to design text (striking, italic, and so forth.).

Use the block manager for more command over happy design.

Add Media:

Embed pictures or mixed media by tapping the "+" button and picking the proper block.

Classifications and Labels:

Appoint applicable classifications and labels to coordinate your substance.

Highlighted Picture:

Set a highlighted picture for visual allure on your post posting.

Save Drafts:

Save your advancement by clicking "Save Draft."

Review:

Review your post to perceive how it will look.

Distribute:

At the point when prepared, click "Distribute" to make your post live.

Permalinks:

Alter the post's permalink for better Website design enhancement.

Website design enhancement Improvement:

Utilize a Search engine optimization module to advance meta titles and depictions.

Make sure to routinely refresh and keep up with your WordPress site for ideal execution.

here are a few extra methods for composing and organizing posts in WordPress:

Headings and Subheadings:

Use headings (H1, H2, and so on) to structure your substance. This further develops meaningfulness and Website design enhancement.

Text Arrangement:

Adjust your text depending on the situation involving the arrangement choices in the toolbar.

Records and List items:

Make requested or unordered records for better association.

Hyperlinks:

Embed hyperlinks by featuring text, tapping the connection symbol, and adding the URL.

Selections:

Create a compact selection to give a synopsis of your post, particularly assuming you're utilizing subjects that show passages.

Peruse More Tag:

For longer posts, consider utilizing the "Read More" tag to show a mystery on the fundamental blog page.

Arranging Statements:

Utilize the blockquote highlight for statements to outwardly recognize them.

Implanting:

Install mixed media, tweets, or other substances utilizing the implant block.

Corrections:

Track changes and corrections in the post utilizing the amendments choice.

Timetable or Draft:

The plan is to be distributed sometime in the not-too-distant future or saved as drafts for future altering.

Portable Streamlining:

Guarantee your substance is versatile for clients on different gadgets.

Edit:

Before distributing, edit your post to avoid any mistakes or blunders.

Remarks and Intelligence:

Energize client commitment by empowering remarks and answering them.

Reinforcement:

Consistently back up your WordPress site to forestall information misfortune.

Custom Fields:

Utilize custom fields to add extra data or metadata to your posts.

Gadgets:

Use gadgets to show explicit substance or highlights in your post sidebar or footer.

Make sure to remain steady with your organizing and style to keep an expert and firm look all through your WordPress site.

Adding Media (Images, Videos)

To add pictures or recordings to WordPress, go to your post/page manager, click on the (+) button, and pick the "Picture" or "Video" block. Then, at that point, transfer your media record or implant the video interface. Change settings and distribute when prepared.

here are more itemized advances:

Pictures:

In the supervisor, click the (+) button to add another block.

Select the "Picture" block.

Transfer your picture or pick one from the media library.

Change picture settings like arrangement, size, and inscription.

Click "Distribute" or "Update" when you're finished.

Recordings:

Utilize the (+) button to add another block.

Pick the "Video" block.

Transfer your video or install it by gluing the video URL.

Change show choices like autoplay and playback controls.

Save or distribute your post/page.

Make sure to see your post to guarantee the media shows up true to form before distributing.

Here's more data:

Media Library:

To deal with your media documents, go to the WordPress dashboard.

Explore "Media" and select "Library."

Here, you can arrange, alter, or erase transferred pictures and recordings.

Picture Displays:

Make a picture display by adding the "Exhibition" block.

Select different pictures to feature together.

Tweak display settings, for example, segments and picture sizes.

Highlighted Pictures:

Set a highlighted picture for your post/page to outwardly address it.

Search for the "Highlighted Picture" choice in the supervisor's sidebar.

Implanting Outside Media:

Reorder the URL of outside media (YouTube, Vimeo, and so on) to insert it straightforwardly into your post/page.

Modifying Picture Sizes:

In the proofreader, you can change picture sizes by choosing a picture and involving the resizing handles or arranging settings in the block toolbar.

Make sure to routinely advance and pack your media for quicker page stacking.

Here are extra tips:

Picture Subtitles and Portrayals:

Use the subtitle and portrayal fields while adding pictures for extra settings or data. This can further develop availability and client experience.

Elective Text (Alt Text):

Continuously add clear alt text to your pictures. This is pivotal for availability and website improvement (Search engine optimization).

Media Arrangement:

Explore different avenues regarding different picture arrangements (left, focus, right) and text wraps to upgrade the visual format of your substance.

Intuitive:

Improve the media transfer process by relocating documents straightforwardly into the proofreader from your PC.

Media Gadgets:

Investigate media gadgets for extra showcase choices, like picture and video sliders or sound playlists.

Picture Altering:

Utilize the inherent picture proofreader to make speedy acclimations to your pictures, such as editing or turning, without leaving the WordPress stage.

Record Arrangements:

WordPress upholds different picture designs (JPEG, PNG, GIF) and video designs (MP4, WebM). Pick the fitting configuration in light of your substance and quality necessities.

Managing Categories and Tags

To oversee classifications and labels in WordPress, go to the "Posts" area in your administrator dashboard. You can add, alter, or erase classifications and labels from the separate choices in the left sidebar. Arrange your substance successfully by doling out important classes and labels to each post.

Here is a more point-by-point breakdown:

Adding Classifications:

Explore the "Posts" segment in the WordPress administrator dashboard.

Click on "Classes" to get to the classification board page.

Enter the new classification name, slug (URL-accommodating rendition), and discretionary parent class if relevant.

Click "Add New Classification" to save.

Altering Classifications:

On the classification board page, find the classification you need to alter and tap on it.

Change the name, slug, or parent class depending on the situation.

Click "Update" to save your changes.

Erasing Classes:

From the class, the board page floats over the class you need to erase.

Click on "Erase" and affirm the activity. Be mindful, as erasing a classification might influence posts related to it.

Adding Labels:

In the "Posts" segment, click on "Labels" to go to the label on the executive's page.

Enter the label name and slug.

Click "Add New Tag" to save.

Altering Labels:

On the label, the executive's page, find the label you need to alter and tap on it.

Change the name or slug on a case-by-case basis.

Click "Update" to save your changes.

Erasing Labels:

Float over the label you need to erase the label on the board page.

Click "Erase" and affirm. Erasing a tag will not erase it from posts; it will eliminate the affiliation.

Keep in mind, that viable utilization of classifications and labels helps in coordinating substance and upgrades the client experience on your WordPress site.

here's more data:

Appointing Classifications and Labels to Posts:

While making or altering a post, you can relegate classifications and labels in the right sidebar under "Classifications" and "Labels" separately.

Select the important classifications and labels that best portray the substance of your post.

Relegating classes and labels sorts out happiness for your perusers and further develops Search engine optimization.

Class and Label Gadgets:

WordPress gives gadgets that show a rundown of classes or labels in your site's sidebar or other widgetized regions.

Explore "Appearance" - > "Gadgets" in the administrator dashboard to add the "Classes" or "Label Cloud" gadget to your ideal gadget region.

Class and Label URLs:

Every class and tag in WordPress has its URL. You can find these URLs by visiting the classification or label the executive's page and tapping on the class or label name.

Use these URLs to make custom menus, route connections, or offer explicit subject files.

Modifying Class and Label Permalinks:

You can alter the construction of the class and tag permalinks under "Settings" - > "Permalinks."

This permits you to make Web optimization well-disposed URLs, improving the general construction of your website.

Mass Altering Classifications and Labels:

In the classification or label of the executive's pages, you can utilize the mass alter choice to all the while rapidly apply changes to different classes or labels.

Here you want to revamp or rename a few classifications or labels.

By successfully overseeing classes and labels, you further develop routes for your site guests as well as upgrade the discoverability of your substance, prompting a more coordinated and easy-to-understand WordPress site.

the following are a couple of extra places:

Classification and Label Portrayals:

You can add depictions to classes and labels to give extra settings to guests.

These depictions can be shown on class and label chronicle pages, offering more data about the subjects.

Classification and Label Connections:

Classifications and labels cooperate, yet they fill various needs. Classes are for the most part utilized for more extensive points, while labels offer more unambiguous subtleties.

Keeping harmony among classifications and labels guarantees an efficient substance structure.

Class and Label Channels in Administrator Screens:

In the posts posting page, you can channel posts in light of classes and labels, making it more straightforward to oversee and view as an unambiguous substance.

Class and Label Best Practices:

Keep your classes and labels reliable and pertinent to your substance.

Try not to make an excessive number of classes or labels, as this can prompt a jumbled construction.

Consistently audit and update your classes and labels to adjust to changes in your substance.

Website design enhancement Contemplations:

Classifications and labels can add to your site's Search engine optimization procedure.

Guarantee that class and label names are unmistakable and incorporate significant watchwords.

Class and Label Modules:

Investigate modules that offer extra elements for overseeing and showing classes and labels.

Some modules give progressed choices for tweaking the showcase of classifications and labels on your site.

Overseeing classes and labels helps with content association as well as upgrades the general client experience and Website optimization execution of your WordPress webpage. Consistently exploring and upgrading your scientific classification can add to the drawn-out progress of your substance procedure.

the following are a couple of additional experiences:

Class and Label Ordered progression:

Classes can be coordinated progressively, permitting you to make parent and kid classifications. This progressive construction adds profundity to your substance association.

Labels, then again, are normally level and don't have a progressive relationship.

Default Classification:

You can set a default classification for your posts. If you neglect to relegate a classification while making a post, it will naturally be doled out to the default classification.

Pick a default classification that lines up with the essential focal point of your substance.

Classification and Label Count:

On the classification and label of the board pages, you can see the number of posts related to every classification or tag.

This count gives a speedy outline of the prominence and importance of your classes and labels.

Class and Label Layouts:

WordPress subjects frequently have layouts for class and label files. These layouts control how the classification and label pages look.

Altering these formats can assist you with fitting the introduction of your chronicle pages to match your site's plan.

Classification and Tag Sidetracks:

If you at any point need to change the slug (URL) of a class or tag, think about setting up sidetracks to keep up with Website optimization and forestall broken joins.

Diverts guarantee that guests who access the old URLs are consequently diverted to the new ones.

High-level Custom Fields with Scientific categorizations:

Some modules and subjects permit you to add custom fields to classes and labels utilizing Progressed Custom Fields or comparable devices.

This can help include extra data or media connected with every class or tag.

Classification and Label Consents:

WordPress permits you to control who can make, alter, and erase classifications and labels. Change these authorizations under "Settings" - > "Expressing" in the administrator dashboard.

Overseeing consent is essential for cooperative substance creation on multi-creator sites.

Keep in mind, that the compelling utilization of classes and labels isn't just about organizing your substance but additionally about making a consistent and coherent route insight for your site guests. Consistently survey and refine your scientific classification to adjust to the developing idea of your substance.

Chapter 3: Customizing Your WordPress Site

Choosing and Installing Themes

To pick and introduce a subject on WordPress, go to your administrator dashboard, explore "Appearance" and afterward "Subjects." Peruse and pick a subject, click "Introduce," and afterward "Enact" to apply it. Guarantee the subject lines up with your site's motivation and is responsive for different gadgets.

Think about subjects with great surveys and customary updates for similarity. Investigate customization choices inside the WordPress Customizer to fit the subject however you would prefer. Make sure to back up your site before significant changes for wellbeing.

While choosing a subject, focus on ones that are improved for speed to upgrade client experience. Check assuming that the topic upholds fundamental modules and is viable with well-known programs.

Investigate premium subjects for extra highlights and devoted help.

Before settling on a subject, survey its demo to figure out its design and highlights. Guarantee the subject is Website design enhancement cordial, as it influences your web page's perceivability in web crawlers. Consistently check for subject updates to keep up with security and usefulness. Moreover, investigate discussions or networks for experiences from different clients.

During subject establishment, deactivate and erase any unused subjects to improve site execution and security. Redo your topic by adding your logo, changing tones, and arranging gadgets. Routinely take a look at your site on various gadgets to guarantee responsiveness. In conclusion, consider your drawn-out needs and versatility while picking a subject.

While introducing a topic, be aware of its effect on page load times. Advance pictures and use reserving modules to upgrade execution. Look into the topic's documentation for investigating and customization tips. Also, join WordPress discussions or networks for important bits of knowledge and help from experienced clients.

Before introducing a subject, survey its help and documentation to guarantee it lines up with your specialized abilities. Assuming that you experience issues, contact the subject engineer or local area for help. Consistently update both your subject and WordPress center to profit from the most recent elements and security patches. Keep a reinforcement of your site to defend your substance in the event of startling issues during subject changes.

Think about the drawn-out supportability of the subject. Pick legitimate subject suppliers or commercial centers to guarantee continuous help and updates. Assess the subject's similarity with well-known modules to improve usefulness. Finally, keep a durable plan by adjusting your picked subject to your image personality and content system.

While choosing a subject, test its presentation utilizing web devices like Google PageSpeed Experiences to guarantee ideal stacking speed. Focus on perfect and efficient topics for better client routes. Remember to review and test your site on different programs to guarantee a reliable encounter for all guests. Routinely survey and update your subject as your site advances to remain current and secure.

Customizing Themes

To redo subjects in WordPress, go to the "Appearance" menu and select "Alter." From that point, you can adjust different components like tones, text styles, and format choices. Explore different avenues regarding the settings to accomplish the ideal search for your site.

Moreover, you can transfer a custom header or foundation picture, change gadget situations, and see changes progressively. Investigate the subject explicit customization choices to fit your WordPress site to your inclinations.

For further developed customization, consider utilizing a youngster subject. This permits you to make code changes without influencing the first subject. You can likewise investigate modules for extra styling choices or counsel the topic's documentation for explicit highlights and settings.

If you're OK with coding, you can get to the subject records straightforwardly using the WordPress supervisor to roll out additional multifaceted improvements. Make sure to back up your site before making any critical changes to stay away from likely issues. Furthermore, remaining refreshed with the most recent WordPress and topic renditions is vital for similarity and security.

To additional upgrade your WordPress subject, consider investigating CSS customization. You can add custom CSS code in the subject customizer to supersede explicit styles or utilize a devoted module for greater adaptability. This permits you to adjust the presence of your site past the choices given in the subject settings.

It is fundamental to Streamline your subject for execution. Pack pictures, influence program reserving, and limit CSS and JavaScript documents. This guarantees your site stacks rapidly, giving a superior client experience. Moreover, routinely take a look at your site's responsiveness on different gadgets to ensure a consistent encounter for all guests.

Routinely refreshing your WordPress subject and modules is urgent for security and usefulness. Consider directing convenience testing to guarantee your site is not difficult to explore, and advance for Website design enhancement by adding significant meta labels and portrayals. Observing site investigation helps track client conduct and illuminates further refinements for a balanced WordPress customization.

While tweaking your WordPress subject, focus on openness highlights. Guarantee your site is usable for everybody, incorporating those with incapacities. Utilize clear alt text for pictures, give console route, and pick discernible text dimensions and varieties. This guarantees a more comprehensive and easy-to-understand insight for all your site guests.

Consider executing a substance system as a component of your WordPress customization. Make drawing in and significant substance consistently to keep your crowd intrigued and draw in new guests. Use modules for Website optimization advancement, virtual entertainment reconciliation, and email advertising to improve your web page's permeability and reach. Consistently survey and update your substance to remain significant and keep a unique web-based presence.

Using Widgets and Menus

Surely! Gadgets and menus are fundamental parts of redoing your WordPress site's appearance and route.

Gadgets:

Go to your WordPress dashboard.

Explore "Appearance" and select "Gadgets."

Simplified gadgets from the passed-on side to gadget-prepared regions on the right (e.g., sidebar or footer).

Arrange gadget settings, like titles or content, depending on the situation.

Menus:

In the WordPress dashboard, go to "Appearance" and pick "Menus."

Make another menu or alter a current one.

Add things like pages, custom connections, or classes to your menu structure.

Put together things by relocating them.

Relegate the menu to a particular area (e.g., essential menu or footer menu).

Save your changes.

This empowers you to control the substance and format of your site, improving client experience and route.

We should dive a piece further:

Gadgets:

Normal Gadgets:

Text: Add custom text or HTML code.

Ongoing Posts: Show a rundown of your most recent blog entries.

Classifications: Show a rundown of post-classes.

Search: Incorporate a hunt bar on your site.

Files: Show a month-to-month chronicle of your posts.

Modifying Gadgets:

Numerous gadgets have settings like titles, several things to show, or explicit substance choices.

A few subjects offer extra gadget regions past the sidebar, as in the header or footer.

Menus:

Making a Menu:

You can make various menus for various areas of your site.

Utilize the "Custom Connections" choice to add outer connections or custom URLs to your menu.

Menu Areas:

Topics characterize different menu areas, like the essential menu, auxiliary menu, or footer menu.

Pick where every menu you make ought to show up on your site.

Super Menus (Progressed):

A few subjects support Uber menus, permitting you to make dropdowns with additional complicated substance structures.

Extra Tips:

Subject Explicit Highlights:

A few topics accompany special gadgets or menu choices, so investigate your subject documentation.

Search for subject customization choices to control tones, textual styles, and design.

Versatile Responsiveness:

Guarantee your picked gadgets and menus function admirably on cell phones for a consistent client experience.

Keep in mind, that the key is to examine and find what turns out best for your site's substance and plan.

We should plunge significantly more profoundly:

High-level Gadget Utilization:

Module Gadgets:

Some modules add their gadgets, similar to virtual entertainment take care of famous posts. Introduce important modules to broaden gadget usefulness.

Investigate gadget permeability choices to control where gadgets seem in light of conditions like page or class.

Custom Gadget Regions:

A few subjects permit you to make custom gadget regions. This is valuable for adding gadgets to explicit areas of your site past the standard areas.

High-level Menu Elements:

Custom Route Walkers:

Engineers can utilize custom route walkers to adjust the result of route menus, taking into account profoundly redid plans.

CSS Classes:

Add custom CSS classes to menu things for more exact styling.

Use the "Screen Choices" tab in the Menus screen to empower extra fields like Connection Target or CSS Classes.

Investigating Tips:

Clashes:

If gadgets or menus aren't acting true to form, check for clashes with subjects or modules by deactivating them individually.

Store:

Clear your program store or any reserving modules to guarantee you're seeing the most recent changes.

Future-Sealing:

Standard Updates:

Keep your WordPress variant, subjects, and modules cutting-edge for security and similarity with the most recent elements.

Kid Topics:

If you anticipate rolling out broad improvements to your subject's plan, consider utilizing a kid subject to protect customizations during topic refreshes.

We should investigate a couple of additional viewpoints:

Gadgets and Website Design Enhancement:

Content Significance:

Guarantee that gadgets enhance your substance and don't divert from your fundamental message. Google values pertinent and easy-to-understand content.

Speed Contemplations:

Inordinate utilization of gadgets can affect your site's stacking speed. Advance pictures and think about languid stacking for better execution.

Menus and Client Experience:

Clear Route:

Structure menus sensibly to direct guests easily through your site. The clear route further develops client experience and assists with Website optimization.

Dropdown Menus:

In the case of utilizing dropdowns, keep them coordinated and simple to explore. Try not to profound home for an easy-to-understand insight, particularly on cell phones.

Availability:

Gadget and Menu Availability:

Guarantee that gadgets and menus are available to clients with handicaps. Utilize clear titles, and appropriate heading designs, and test with availability apparatuses.

Alt Text for Pictures:

Assuming your gadgets incorporate pictures, add distinct alt text for openness and Web optimization benefits.

Investigation Reconciliation:

Following Gadget and Menu Cooperations:

Incorporate Google Examination or other investigation apparatuses to follow how clients collaborate with your gadgets and menus. This information can assist you with refining your site's design.

Web-based Entertainment Mix:

Web-based Entertainment Gadgets:

Incorporate web-based entertainment gadgets to empower sharing and associate your website with your social presence.

Menu Connects to Social Profiles:

In your menus, consider adding connections to your online entertainment profiles for simple access.

Keep in mind, that the objective is to make a site that is both easy to use and lined up with your substance procedure.

Chapter 4: Essential Plugins

Introduction to Plugins

In WordPress, modules are bits of programming that add explicit elements or functionalities to your site. They upgrade the center's usefulness without modifying the WordPress center records. Modules can go from basic instruments to complex applications, permitting clients to tweak and expand their locales easily. To introduce a module, explore the WordPress dashboard, go to "Modules," and snap "Add New." From that point, you can look for, introduce, and enact modules in light of your site's necessities.

Once enacted, modules coordinate flawlessly with your WordPress site, showing up in the administrator menu. You can arrange their settings, and update or deactivate them depending on the situation. Modules can fill different needs, like Website design enhancement advancement, security improvements, online business functionalities, or web-based entertainment reconciliation. It's critical to pick trustworthy modules from the WordPress Module Index, as inadequately coded or obsolete ones might affect your site's presentation and security. Routinely refreshing modules guarantees similarity with the most recent WordPress variant and keeps a solid site.

WordPress modules are many times created by different local areas of engineers, going from people to organizations. Some famous modules incorporate Yoast Web optimization for site design improvement, WooCommerce for a web-based business, and Jetpack for a set-up of website the executive's instruments. Clients can likewise make custom modules custom-fitted to their particular requirements. Understanding the motivation behind each module, investigating client evaluations, and checking similarity with your WordPress adaptation are fundamental contemplations while choosing and overseeing modules. Remember that while modules can upgrade usefulness, an unreasonable number might affect site speed, so it's fitting to just introduce what is fundamental for your site's goals.

It's fundamental to consistently refresh your modules to guarantee similarity with the most recent WordPress rendition and to profit from security patches and new elements. In any case, before refreshing, it's wise to make a reinforcement of your site to forestall any possible issues. Also, be mindful of module clashes - some modules may not function admirably together, causing surprising blunders. Testing new modules on an organizing site or during non-top hours can help you recognize and determine clashes without influencing your live site. In general, a smart and key way to deal with modules on the board adds to a protected, effective, and easily working WordPress site.

While modules offer strong functionalities, focusing on higher expectations without ever compromising is significant. A very much-kept-up-with, routinely refreshed module is bound to give a steady and secure insight for your site. Continuously read client surveys and documentation before introducing a module to figure out its standing and similarity. Furthermore, think about the drawn-out help and responsiveness of the module's engineer, as dynamic support guarantees continuous similarity with WordPress refreshes. Routinely review your modules and deactivate or eliminate any that are as of now not important to limit potential security gambles and smooth out your site's exhibition.

While creating custom arrangements or investigating issues, understanding the WordPress Module Programming interface can be valuable. The Module Programming interface gives snares and channels that permit designers to cooperate with different parts of WordPress, empowering them to alter and broaden their usefulness. Figuring out how to make your modules or adjust existing ones can engage you to fit your site exactly to your requirements. Using coding norms and best practices guarantees the unwavering quality and similarity of your modules, adding to a vigorous and effective WordPress environment.

It's significant that while modules are a useful asset, they ought to be utilized sensibly to try not to overburden your site. Unnecessary modules can influence execution, prompting more slow burden times. Consistently screen your site's speed and consider utilizing apparatuses like reserving modules to upgrade execution. Moreover, remain informed about security best practices, as modules can be a potential passage point for weaknesses. In outline, a reasonable way to deal with module utilization, combined with standard support and security checks, adds to a sound and successful WordPress site.

Installing and Activating Plugins

To introduce and actuate modules in WordPress:

Sign in to your WordPress administrator dashboard.

Explore the "Modules" menu on the left sidebar.

Click on "Add New."

Utilize the pursuit bar to find a particular module or peruse accessible modules.

When you find the ideal module, click "Introduce Now."

After establishment, click "Enact" to actuate the module.

Make sure to pick trustworthy modules and keep them refreshed for security and usefulness.

Here is a smidgen more detail:

Investigate the "Introduced Modules" segment to oversee and arrange your enacted modules.

Some modules might require extra settings. Search for a committed menu or settings connected with the introduced module.

Routinely update your modules to guarantee similarity with the most recent WordPress form and keep up with security.

Be mindful of the number of modules you introduce, as too many can affect your site's exhibition. Pick just fundamental and all-around kept up with modules.

The following are a couple of extra tips:

Deactivating and Erasing: If you want to deactivate or eliminate a module, go to the "Modules" page, find the pertinent module, and pick the fitting activity - all things considered "Deactivate" or "Erase."

Manual Establishment: For modules not accessible in the WordPress Module Registry, you might have to transfer them physically. Utilize the "Transfer Module" choice on the "Add New" page.

Investigating: If a module causes issues, deactivate it to check if the issue continues to happen. You can then investigate or look for help for the clashing module.

Reinforcement Your Site: Before major module establishments or updates, it's prudent to back up your WordPress site. This guarantees you can return to a steady state if any issues emerge.

Look at Similarity: Confirm that the modules you need to introduce are viable with your WordPress form. Designers for the most part notice this data in the module subtleties.

Security Contemplations: Just download modules from dependable sources to keep away from security gambles. Understand audits, really look at appraisals, and guarantee the module is effectively kept up with.

here are a few extra crucial subtleties:

Module Updates: Consistently check for refreshes for all your modules. Designers discharge updates to further develop usefulness, fix bugs, and upgrade security.

Module Similarity: Guarantee that the modules you pick are viable with your WordPress rendition as well as with other modules you're utilizing. Similarity issues can prompt glitches.

Module Documentation: Audit the documentation given by module engineers. It frequently remembers significant data for how to utilize the module really and investigate normal issues.

Execution Observing: Screen your site's presentation after putting in new modules. Some modules could influence site speed, so use apparatuses like GTmetrix or Google PageSpeed Experiences to survey execution.

Consents: Be aware of the authorization modules require. Just award fundamental consent to keep up with the security of your site.

Client Surveys: Before introducing a module, read client audits and evaluations. They can offer bits of knowledge about the client's experience and potential difficulties others have confronted.

Multisite Contemplations: If you're running a WordPress Multisite establishment, check if the module is viable with Multisite and if it should be network-enacted or initiated on individual destinations.

Keep in mind that a very much oversaw module climate adds to a protected, productive, and practical WordPress site.

Must-Have Plugins for Beginners

For WordPress novices, fundamental modules include:

Yoast Website design enhancement: Advance your webpage for web indexes.

Akismet: Safeguard against spam remarks.

Jetpack: Gives different highlights like site details, security, and social sharing.

UpdraftPlus: Reinforcement your site without any problem.

Elementor: Fabricate pages outwardly with an intuitive supervisor.

W3 All-out Reserve: Further develop site speed and execution.

Wordfence Security: Improve site security with firewall and malware examination.

Contact Structure 7: Make straightforward contact structures.

Smush: Pack and streamline pictures for quicker stacking.

WPForms: Effectively assemble different structures for your site.

Make sure to consistently refresh and survey module similarity for a smooth WordPress experience.

the following are a couple of more modules for WordPress novices:

MonsterInsights: Incorporate Google Investigation for nitty gritty site examination.

WP Super Reserve: Another storing module to upgrade site speed.

Truly Straightforward SSL: Effectively secure your site with an SSL authentication.

Sucuri Security: Adds a layer of safety with observing and malware filtering.

Redirection: Oversee 301 sidetracks for further developed Website design enhancement and client experience.

ShortPixel Picture Streamlining agent: Pack and improve pictures without forfeiting quality.

Exemplary Proofreader: Assuming that you favor the old manager, this module reestablishes the exemplary WordPress supervisor.

Social Symbols Gadget and Block by WPZOOM: Add upscale online entertainment symbols to your website.

OneSignal Pop-up messages: Draw in guests with message pop-ups for new satisfaction.

Simple Chapter-by-chapter guide: Produce a chapter-by-chapter guide for long articles or pages.

Continuously be careful not to over-burden your site with such a large number of modules, as it might influence execution.

the following are a couple of extra modules for WordPress novices:

Broken Connection Checker: Distinguish and fix broken joins on your site.

AMP for WP - Sped up Portable Pages: Work on versatile involvement in quicker stacking AMP pages.

TablePress: Make and oversee tables effectively for your substance.

Elementor Addons and Layouts - Sizzify Light: Upgrade Elementor with extra gadgets and formats.

Flourish Engineer: A strong page manufacturer with change-centered components.

Cripple Remarks: Effectively switch off remarks on unambiguous post types or all through your site.

Truly Basic SSL: Consequently distinguish and design SSL settings for a solid site.

WP Mail SMTP by WPForms: Guarantee dependable email conveyance by designing SMTP settings.

Across the board Mapping Rich Bits: Work on your site's appearance in list items with rich scraps.

Make sure to consistently refresh your modules and screen their effect on nearby execution and security.

Chapter 5: Managing Users and Comments

User Roles and Permissions

In WordPress, client jobs characterize the abilities and consents allowed to clients. Normal jobs incorporate Executive, Proofreader, Writer, Donor, and Supporter. Chairmen have full control, Editors oversee content, Creators can distribute their posts, Benefactors can submit posts yet not distribute, and Supporters can deal with their profiles. You can modify jobs utilizing modules for additional particular authorizations.

To alter client jobs in WordPress, explore the "Clients" segment in the administrator dashboard. You can add or alter clients, allotting jobs appropriately. Modules like "Individuals" or "Client Job Supervisor" give progressed customization, permitting you to make new jobs or tweak abilities for existing ones. It's urgent to relegate jobs given the errands clients need to perform to keep a safe and coordinated site.

Also, understanding the abilities related to every job is fundamental. For instance, chairmen can introduce modules and change subjects, while editors can oversee content but not adjust site settings. Routinely survey and update client jobs to guarantee proper access levels and upgrade the general security of your WordPress site. Use job-the-board modules to smooth out this interaction and keep a very organized client pecking order.

Consider carrying out two-factor verification for added security, paying little mind to client jobs. This additional layer of insurance improves the general security of your WordPress site by expecting clients to give a second type of check, typically through a cell phone or email. Consistently review client records and authorizations to repudiate access for idle or superfluous clients, lessening potential security gambles. Keeping your WordPress establishment, subjects, and modules modern is critical for keeping a solid climate.

Besides, if you want to give transitory access or explicit consent to a client, WordPress upholds capacities like custom client jobs and abilities. This permits you to fit admittance freedoms to explicit necessities, guaranteeing clients have unequivocally the consent expected for their assignments without compromising site security. Routinely speak with your colleagues about their jobs and obligations to ensure an unmistakable comprehension of the entrance they have and the activities they can perform on the WordPress site.

It's fitting to areas of strength for utilization, passwords for every client account, and energize customary secret phrase refreshes. Utilizing security modules, like Wordfence or Sucuri, can add a layer of assurance by checking and obstructing dubious exercises. Furthermore, consider restricting login endeavors to upset potential animal power assaults. Routinely backing up your WordPress site is significant for speedy recuperation in the event of any security episodes or information misfortune. Consistently survey logs and security reports to remain informed about expected weaknesses and go to proactive lengths to address them.

While managing client jobs, guarantee that content control lines up with your site's principles. Editors can direct and oversee content, yet characterizing rules and executing article work processes can keep up with consistency. For participation locales or those with confined content, modules like "MemberPress" or "Limit Content Expert" can assist with controlling access in light of client jobs and memberships. Consistently observing client action and site logs recognizes and addresses any dubious way of behaving expeditiously. Steady observing and proactive safety efforts add to a vigorous and secure WordPress climate.

Dealing with Comments

Overseeing remarks in WordPress includes exploring the "Remarks" segment in the administrator dashboard. There, you can support, alter, mark as spam, or erase remarks. Use settings to direct remarks before they show up, improving command over your site's conversation.

You can redo remark settings in WordPress under "Settings" > "Conversation." Pick choices like requiring balance for first-time analysts, setting a remark boycott, or empowering strung remarks for better association. Consistently check and draw in with remarks to encourage a solid local area on your site.

Consider introducing modules like Akismet to consequently channel and block spam remarks. Moreover, support client connection by answering remarks, which can help commitment and make a feeling of the local area on your WordPress site. Routinely update your WordPress establishment and modules to improve security and remark on the board highlights.

Whenever overpowered with remarks, you can execute pagination or use instruments to show remarks in light of specific measures. Support a positive climate by laying out clear remark rules. At last, screen client-produced content to guarantee it lines up with your site's strategies and norms.

To additional upgrade remark the executives, influence client jobs to allocate explicit honors. You can allot jobs like "Director," "Proofreader," or "Arbitrator" to people answerable for regulating and answering remarks. This adds a layer of control and conveys liabilities.

Consider coordinating web-based entertainment remarking frameworks like Disqus or Facebook Remarks to widen the conversation reach. These frameworks frequently smooth out the remarking system and give extra control highlights. Also, consistently survey and update your remark control rules to adjust to changing local area elements and assumptions.

Investigate utilizing the "Answer" and "Like" highlights inside WordPress remarks to draw in your crowd effectively. This cultivates a feeling of the local area and supports further conversation. Watch out for input investigation if accessible, as it can give experiences into which posts produce more cooperation, assisting you with fitting your substance system.

Chapter 6 SEO Basics for WordPress

Understanding SEO

Web optimization in WordPress includes enhancing your site to work on its permeability on web crawlers. Utilize significant watchwords, make quality substance, enhance meta labels, and guarantee a versatile plan. Furthermore, consider utilizing Website design enhancement modules like Yoast to help with on-page improvement. Routinely update content, form quality backlinks, and screen your site's presentation to upgrade its Website design enhancement.

The following are a couple of additional ways to figure out Web optimization in WordPress:

Quality Substance: Make significant, applicable, and connecting content. Routinely update your site with new material to draw in the two clients and web search tools.

Permalinks: Use Web optimization cordial permalinks. Pick a design that incorporates watchwords and makes your URLs lucid. You can redo permalinks in the WordPress settings.

Picture Streamlining: Pack and upgrade pictures to lessen record sizes without compromising quality. Utilize unmistakable document names and alt text to assist with looking through motors to grasp the substance of your pictures.

Sitemap and Robots.txt: Present a sitemap to web search tools, and design your robots.txt record to direct web search tool crawlers on what parts of your webpage to slither and list.

Interior Connecting: Connection to applicable inner pages inside your substance. This appropriates interface value and upgrades the general construction of your site.

Responsive Plan: Guarantee your site is dynamic. Google thinks about versatile similarity as a positioning component, so having a responsive plan is critical for Website optimization.

Virtual Entertainment Incorporation: Offer your substance via web-based entertainment stages to expand permeability and drive traffic. Social signs may by implication influence web crawler rankings.

Page Speed Streamlining: Further develop your site's stacking speed. Use storing modules, streamline pictures, and consider a solid facilitating supplier to improve the general presentation.

SSL Testament: Introduce an SSL declaration to guarantee your site is served over HTTPS. Google thinks about secure destinations as a positive positioning element.

Client Experience (UX): Make an easy-to-understand insight. A clear route, simple-to-understand content, and an efficient site structure add to better client commitment, which can emphatically influence Search engine optimization.

Keep in mind that web optimization is a continuous cycle, and remaining informed about industry changes and patterns is pivotal for keeping up with and further developing your site's web search tool permeability.

The following are a couple of further developed Website optimization tips for WordPress:

Blueprint Markup: Carry out diagram markup to give web Indexes organized data about your substance. This can improve how your pages show up in query items, possibly expanding navigate rates.

Sanctioned URLs: Utilize standard labels to stay away from copy-content issues. Determine the favored form of a page to assist with looking through motors to comprehend which rendition to file.

Hreflang Labels: On the off chance that your site has various language variants or targets various districts, use Hreflang labels to show the language and provincial focus of each page.

301 Sidetracks: Appropriately set up 301 sidetracks for any changed URLs. This guarantees that web crawlers and clients are diverted to the right and refreshed page.

Custom Portions: Art extraordinary and convincing meta depictions for each page. While not an immediate positioning element, an elegantly composed meta depiction can tempt clients to tap on your connection in list items.

Organized Information: Influence organized information to give web indexes more point-by-point data about your substance. This can upgrade rich bits and work on the introduction of your substance in list items.

XML Sitemaps: Consistently update and present your XML sitemap to web search tools. This assists them with finding new happiness and grasping the design of your site.

Screen and Examine: Use devices like Google Investigation and Google Search Control Center to screen your site's presentation. Examine client conduct, track catchphrase rankings, and address any issues that might emerge.

Content Storehouses: Arrange your substance into topical storehouses or classifications. This assists web indexes with grasping the effective importance of your substance and can further develop the by and large Search engine optimization construction of your website.

Client-Created Content: Empower client-produced content like surveys or remarks. This can add new, significant substance to your site and increment client commitment.

Keep in mind that website optimization techniques can differ in light of your particular objectives and industry. Consistently review and adjust your way of dealing with lineup with best practices and changes in web search tool calculations.

Optimizing Content for Search Engines

To upgrade content for web search tools in WordPress:

Utilize a Search engine optimization module like Yoast or Rank Math to set meta titles and portrayals.

Incorporate important catchphrases normally in your substance.

Improve pictures with graphic alt text.

Make a sitemap and submit it to web indexes utilizing the Google Search Control Center.

Guarantee your site has a perfect, versatile plan.

Further, develop page stacking speed; consider utilizing a storing module.

Utilize inner connecting to associate-related content.

Routinely update and add new, great substance.

Support client commitment through remarks and social sharing.

Screen your site's presentation utilizing examination apparatuses.

Carry out clean and Website optimization agreeable URLs. Pick compact and pertinent slugs for your posts and pages.

Use header labels (H1, H2, and so on) to structure your substance and feature central issues for web crawlers.

Research and dissect your main interest group's pursuit aim to adjust your substance to their questions.

Secure your site with HTTPS to acquire a slight positioning lift and further develop client trust.

Upgrade your site for neighborhood search by including area-based catchphrases and making a Google My Business profile.

Support backlinks from trustworthy sources to upgrade your site's power and believability.

Consistently check for and fix broken joins on your site to keep a positive client experience.

Influence web-based entertainment to advance your substance, as friendly signs can in a roundabout way influence search rankings.

Screen and address any Search engine optimization issues hailed by your picked Website design enhancement module or different devices.

Remain refreshed on Search engine optimization patterns and calculation changes to as needs adjust your procedure.

Direct watchword exploration to recognize high-esteem terms for your specialty and coordinate them decisively into your substance.

Streamline your WordPress site's permalinks design to make URLs that are both easy to understand and Website optimization amicable.

Center around making top-caliber, shareable substance that normally draws in inbound connections from different sites.

Guarantee your site is portable and receptive to take care of the developing number of clients getting to content on cell phones.

Use mapping markup to give web search tools organized information, upgrading the showcase of your substance in query items.

Consistently review and update obsolete substances to keep them significant and keep up with web index permeability.

Execute a responsive and easy-to-use plan to upgrade the general client experience on your site.

Use header labels fittingly, involving H1 for fundamental titles and organizing happy with H2, H3, and so on, for subheadings.

Urge and answer client surveys, particularly if your site includes items or administrations, as they can affect nearby hunt rankings.

Influence Google Examination to acquire experiences in client conduct, assisting you with refining your substance technique in light of crowd inclinations.

Add clear and convincing meta titles and meta portrayals to tempt clients to tap on your query items.

Pack pictures to decrease record measures and further develop page stacking times, adding to a superior client experience.

Use a reserving module to store static renditions of your site, diminishing server burden and accelerating page load times.

Empower program reserving to permit guests to store components of your site locally, further improving stacking speed.

Consistently check for and fix copy content issues to keep away from potential Web optimization punishments.

Use a dependable facilitating supplier to guarantee your site's exhibition and uptime are reliably high.

Improve your WordPress site for voice search by making content that answers normal language inquiries compactly.

Execute 301 sidetracks for any changed URLs to keep up with connect value and keep clients from experiencing broken joins

Influence social confirmation, for example, tributes and client-produced content, to construct trust and believability with your crowd.

Watch out for your webpage's general security, as secure sites are frequently preferred via web search tools. Routinely update modules and subjects, and consider a security module.

Routinely check and work on the meaningfulness of your substance, guaranteeing it is effectively reasonable for the two clients and web crawlers.

Use Google's Inquiry Control Center to distinguish and fix slither mistakes, guaranteeing web search tools can appropriately file your website.

Advance your site's pictures by utilizing expressive record names and adding alt text, assisting web indexes with grasping their substance.

Use web-based entertainment sharing buttons on your website to urge clients to share your substance, possibly expanding its permeability.

Carry out a responsive plan that changes consistently to various screen sizes, further developing the client experience on different gadgets.

Exploration and utilize long-tail catchphrases to target more unambiguous inquiry questions and draw in a specialty crowd.

Influence video content, as it can upgrade client commitment and add to the more likely web search tool rankings.

Use header labels to make various leveled structures for your substance, making it more intelligible and open.

Routinely screen and further develop your site's general client experience, as sure client signs can influence search rankings.

Remain informed about the most recent Website optimization patterns and calculation updates to adjust your technique and keep up with ideal web index permeability.

Using SEO Plugins

Without a doubt, improving your WordPress site for web indexes is significant. Famous Search engine optimization modules like Yoast Website Design Enhancement or Across the Board Search Engine Optimization Pack can assist you with overseeing titles, meta portrayals, and XML sitemaps, and that's only the tip of the iceberg. Introduce the module, follow arrangement prompts, and use elements to improve your site's Web optimization.

Inside Website design enhancement modules, center around catchphrase advancement, lucidness examination, and making Search engine optimization cordial URLs. Use highlights like picture streamlining and virtual entertainment mix to improve generally speaking permeability. Consistently update content and remain informed about Website optimization best practices for supported improvement.

Moreover, influences the Search engine optimization module for cutting edge settings like standard URLs, 301 sidetracks, and construction markup. Screen investigation to follow execution and change techniques likewise. Reliable substance updates and top-notch backlinks are key for long-haul Web optimization achievement.

Consider streamlining your site's speed and portable responsiveness, as these are factors web indexes focus on. Use the module's elements for making an XML sitemap to assist with looking through motors slither and record your substance proficiently. Remain informed about calculation updates to likewise adjust your Website optimization procedure.

Use the Web optimization module's instruments for recognizing and fixing broken joins. Executing legitimate header labels and keeping a spotless site structure adds to better Website design enhancement. Consistently review and update your substance to guarantee it stays important and lines up with ebb and flow search patterns. Draw in with your crowd through remarks and web-based entertainment for expanded permeability.

Investigate the module's highlights for breaking down contenders' catchphrases and procedures. Use the module's ideas for working on your substance's lucidness and in general client experience. Consistently survey and update your site's permalink structure for Search engine optimization agreeable URLs. Make sure to present your sitemap to web crawlers for better ordering.

center around building areas of strength for a connecting design to upgrade routes and circulate interface value across your site. Use the Web optimization module's instruments for observing and overseeing 404 mistakes. Routinely check and enhance your site's robots.txt record to control web search tool crawlers' admittance to explicit pieces of your webpage.

Investigate the module's highlights for enhancing pictures, including legitimate alt text and record names. Use the breadcrumb route to improve client experience and web crawler comprehension of your website's design. Routinely check for and fix any copy content issues that might emerge. Participate in moral external link establishment practices to work on your site's power.

Chapter 7: Security Best Practices

Securing Your WordPress Site

Getting your WordPress site is pivotal. Begin by keeping programming, subjects, and modules refreshed to fix weaknesses. Utilize solid, one-of-a-kind passwords, execute two-factor confirmation, and consistently back up your site. Consider a security module, limit login endeavors, and screen client action. Also, incapacitating catalog posting and consistently reviewing clients represents superfluous access.

 Find these extra ways to improve WordPress security:

Pick a Safe Facilitating Supplier:
Decide on a trustworthy facilitating supplier that focuses on security and gives highlights like firewalls, customary reinforcements, and malware checking.
SSL Encryption:
Empower SSL (Secure Attachment Layer) to scramble information transmission between your site and clients. This guarantees a safe association, particularly during login and installment processes.

Limit Login Endeavors:

Carry out limitations on the number of login endeavors to forestall beast force assaults. Numerous security modules offer this component.

Safeguard wp-config.php:

Secure the wp-config.php record by moving it to a more elevated level index than the default. This adds a layer of assurance against unapproved access.

Cripple XML-RPC:

On the off chance that you don't utilize XML-RPC usefulness, think about debilitating it, as it tends to be taken advantage of for DDoS assaults. Security modules frequently incorporate a choice to impair XML-RPC.

Eliminate Unused Topics and Modules:

Uninstall any topics or modules that you're not utilizing. They can be potential section focuses for assailants while perhaps not consistently refreshed.

Document Authorizations:

Set appropriate record authorizations on your WordPress establishment. Limit admittance to fundamental documents and indexes to limit the gamble of unapproved adjustments.

Security Modules:

Consider utilizing respectable security modules like Wordfence or Sucuri. These instruments offer highlights like firewall insurance, malware checking, and constant danger observation.

Standard Reinforcements:

Plan standard reinforcements of your site, including data sets and records. This guarantees you can rapidly reestablish your site if there's a security occurrence.

Screen Client Movement:

Watch out for client movement. On the off chance that you have various clients, allot proper jobs and consistently review their consents to forestall unapproved access.

Keep in mind, that security is a continuous cycle. Routinely audit and update your safety efforts to remain in front of developing dangers.

here are a few extra measures to brace your WordPress site:

Content Conveyance Organization (CDN):

Executing a CDN can upgrade security by circulating your site's static substance across different servers worldwide, decreasing the gamble of DDoS assaults and further developing burden times.

Web Application Firewall (WAF):

Consider utilizing an Internet Application Firewall to channel and screen HTTP traffic between your webpage and the Web. WAFs can help safeguard against different web-based dangers, including SQL infusion and cross-website prearranging.

Deny Catalog Posting:

Guarantee that registry posting is debilitated to keep aggressors from effectively getting a rundown of records in your catalogs. This is ordinarily finished by including "Choices - Records" in your site's .htaccess document.

Information base Security:

Change the default information base table prefix from "wp_" to something exceptional during the WordPress establishment process. This adds a layer of intricacy for assailants attempting to take advantage of information base weaknesses.

Standard Security Reviews:

Direct occasional security reviews of your WordPress site. Search for weaknesses, obsolete programming, and any dubious exercises. Security modules can robotize a portion of these checks.

Solidify wp-administrator Access:

Confine admittance to the wp-administrator index by restricting it to explicit IP addresses. This can be accomplished through your site's .htaccess record or with security modules.

Security Headers:

Carry out security headers like Substance Security Strategy (CSP), Severe Vehicle Security (HSTS), and X-Content-Type-Choices. These headers improve program security and safeguard against different kinds of assaults.

Incapacitate Registry Posting:

Ensure that catalog posting is crippled to keep aggressors from effectively getting a rundown of records in your registries. This is regularly finished by including "Choices - Records" in your site's .htaccess document.

Instruct Clients:

Train clients with admittance to your WordPress site about security best practices. Guarantee they grasp the significance of solid passwords, stay away from dubious connections, and reveal any uncommon exercises expeditiously.

Remain Informed:

Keep yourself refreshed on WordPress security news and weaknesses. Buy into security mailing records and follow trustworthy security sites to remain informed about arising dangers and best practices.

Executing a mix of these actions will fundamentally upgrade the security of your WordPress site. Routinely survey and adjust your security system as the danger scene develops.

how about we dive into some extra high-level safety efforts for your WordPress site:

Use Security Headers:

Utilize security headers like Substance Security Strategy (CSP) and HTTP Severe Vehicle Security (HSTS) to add a layer of assurance against different kinds of assaults, including cross-site prearranging (XSS) and man-in-the-center assaults.

Execute a Subresource Respectability (SRI):

Use SRI to guarantee that outer assets (e.g., scripts, templates) stacked by your site haven't been altered. This keeps assailants from infusing noxious code into your site through compromised outside assets.

Information base Table Prefix:

While changing the information base table prefix during establishment is a decent beginning, consider doing it physically before establishment for added security. Randomize the prefix to make it more trying for aggressors.

Cripple PHP Execution in Untrusted Organizers:

In registries where it's excessive, handicap PHP execution to forestall potential code infusion assaults. This can accomplished by adding "Choices - ExecCGI" to your site's .htaccess document in unambiguous catalogs.

Security Headers for Login Pages:

Apply extra security headers explicitly for your login pages. This can help safeguard against assaults focusing on your login structures, for example, savage power endeavors or qualification stuffing.

WordPress Salts and Keys:

Consistently update your WordPress salts and keys in the wp-config.php document. These are cryptographic keys used to work on the encryption of data put away in client threats, adding a layer of safety.

Detach WordPress Setup:

Detach the wp-config.php and .htaccess records by moving them to a more significant level catalog outside the root organizer. This limits the gamble of unapproved access or double-dealing.

Record Framework Security:

Routinely review and secure document consents. Guarantee that documents and catalogs are set to the base vital consents for legitimate usefulness, diminishing the potential for unapproved access.

HTTP Security Headers:

Design HTTP security headers, like X-Edge Choices and X-Content-Type Choices, to control how

programs handle your site's substance. This forestalls clickjacking and Emulate-type sniffing.
Screen Record Changes:
Use record respectability observing instruments to monitor changes to your WordPress documents. Any startling changes can be an indication of a security break, and early discovery is pivotal.
Carrying out these high-level safety efforts will altogether improve the heartiness of your WordPress site's guards. Consistently reevaluate and refresh your security procedure to remain in front of arising dangers.

Regular Backups

Standard reinforcements are pivotal for WordPress sites. Utilize a dependable reinforcement module, plan robotized reinforcements, and store duplicates offsite for added security.

Consider a reinforcement recurrence that lines up with your substance refreshes. Modules like UpdraftPlus or Jetpack offer easy-to-understand choices for booked reinforcements. Guarantee your reinforcement records are put away on cloud administrations like Dropbox or Google Drive to defend against server disappointments. Testing your reinforcement reclamation process occasionally is likewise fitting to ensure a speedy recuperation if necessary.

remember both information base and record reinforcements for your daily schedule to cover all parts of your WordPress site. Record your reinforcement techniques, including the area and access subtleties, to smooth out recuperation endeavors. Ultimately, remain careful for module refreshes, as similarity issues can at times influence reinforcement processes.

Execute a complete reinforcement technique by joining customary robotized reinforcements with infrequent manual reinforcements before significant updates or changes. Confirm that your reinforcement arrangement upholds gradual reinforcements to save extra room. Make sure to consistently survey and tidy up more established reinforcements to forestall pointless messes and improve stockpiling proficiency.

Consider a three-duplicate reinforcement rule: one on the server, one on an alternate server, and one disconnected. This limits gambles and guarantees information accessibility. Investigate reinforcement arrangements with worked-in highlights for encryption to upgrade the security of your put-away reinforcements. Finally, consistently screen your reinforcement interaction for any disappointments or inconsistencies to expeditiously resolve issues.

Occasionally check the respectability of your reinforcement documents to guarantee they are not undermined. If your facilitating supplier offers server-level reinforcements, it's smart to enhance those with your autonomous reinforcements for added overt repetitiveness. Keep your WordPress center, subjects, and modules modern to upgrade the general security of your site and work on the unwavering quality of your reinforcements.

Consider utilizing a variant control framework like Git for your WordPress site, particularly for custom code. This gives an extra layer of control and permits you to follow changes over the long run. Moreover, execute a debacle recuperation plan, framing bit-by-bit methodology to continue if there should be an occurrence of a significant site issue, guaranteeing a quick and compelling reaction. Consistently return to and update your reinforcement technique as your site develops to remain lined up with its evolving needs.

Broaden capacity areas for your reinforcements, utilizing a blend of cloud administrations and nearby stockpiling to limit chances. Keep documentation of your reinforcement and recuperation process open to pertinent colleagues, guaranteeing progression in the event of workforce changes. At long last, instruct yourself on the points of interest of your picked reinforcement arrangement, understanding its restrictions and abilities to settle on informed choices concerning your WordPress site's information security.

Updates and Maintenance

Standard updates and upkeep are urgent for a WordPress site. Guarantee you:

Center Updates: Keep WordPress center, subjects, and modules refreshed to the most recent renditions for security and execution upgrades.

Reinforcement: Consistently reinforce your site to stay away from information misfortune. Use modules or your facilitating supplier's instruments for this.

Security: Carry out safety efforts, for example, solid passwords, SSL declarations, and security modules. Consistently check for malware.

Data set Streamlining: Advance your data set consistently to further develop site speed. Modules like WP-Improve can assist with this.

Broken Connections: Check and fix broken connections to keep a positive client experience and Website optimization.

Picture Enhancement: Pack pictures to lessen page load times. Use modules like Smush or Imagify.

Reserving: Empower storing to improve site speed. W3 All-out Reserve or WP Super Store are well-known modules for this.

Audit Client Access: Consistently survey and update client jobs and consents to guarantee the right access levels.

Take a look at Structures: If you have contact structures, test them occasionally to guarantee they're working accurately.

Screen Execution: Use instruments like Google PageSpeed Bits of Knowledge or GTmetrix to screen and further develop site execution.

Survey and Erase Unused Topics/Modules: Decrease security gambles by eliminating any pointless subjects or modules.

By consistently playing out these errands, you can keep your WordPress site secure, improved, and moving along as expected.

Here are extra tips for WordPress updates and support:

Content Survey: Consistently audit and update your substance. Guarantee data is precise, and eliminates obsolete or unessential substance.

Look at Versatile Responsiveness: Test your site's responsiveness on different gadgets to guarantee a consistent client experience.

Screen Remarks: Assuming that you permit remarks, moderate and answer them immediately.

Consider utilizing spam modules to sift through spam remarks.

Screen Site Investigation: Use apparatuses like Google Examination to follow site traffic, client conduct, and other important bits of knowledge for key choices.

SSL Recharging: Guarantee your SSL endorsement is forward-thinking and reestablished before lapse to keep a solid association.

Availability: Make your site open to all clients. Check for consistency with availability principles and make essential changes.

DNS and Facilitating Survey: Routinely audit your DNS settings and facilitate the foundation for any expected issues. Guarantee your facilitating plan meets your ongoing requirements.

Overt repetitiveness and Reinforcements: Consider executing overt repetitiveness gauges, and check that your reinforcement framework is working accurately.

Test Site Speed: Routinely test your site's speed and streamline it further if necessary. A quicker site further develops client experience and Web optimization.

Remain Informed: Keep yourself refreshed on WordPress news, security issues, and best practices. Buy into solid hotspots for convenient data.

Recall that ordinary, proactive support forestalls issues and keeps your WordPress site in top condition.

here are a few extra tips for WordPress updates and support:

Custom Code Audit: Assuming you've executed custom code, survey and update it consistently to guarantee similarity with the most recent WordPress adaptations.

Look at Cross-Program Similarity: Test your site across different programs to guarantee a steady encounter for all clients.

404 Blunder Checking: Screen and address 404 mistakes by utilizing devices or modules to divert broken connections and keep a smooth route insight.

Update PHP Variant: Stay up with the latest for better execution and security. Guarantee similarity with your topics and modules.

Legitimate Consistence: Routinely audit and update your site's protection strategy, terms of administration, and some other authoritative records to follow guidelines.

Email Deliverability: Assuming that your site sends messages (e.g., contact structure notices), guarantee legitimate email deliverability by arranging SMTP settings or utilizing respectable email administrations.

Website streamlining (Web optimization): Improve your substance for web search tools, update meta labels, and consider making a sitemap to assist with looking through motors files on your website successfully.

Client Experience (UX) Audit: Occasionally evaluate the general client experience, including route, plan, and format, and make enhancements appropriately.

Survey Client Criticism: If clients give input, think about it and make improvements to address their ideas or concerns.

Crisis Plan: Have an emergency course of action for crises, including a new reinforcement and contact data for your facilitating supplier.

Team up Safely: Assuming you have various givers, guarantee they follow the best security rehearses and have the essential consents without superfluous access.

By integrating these practices into your WordPress support schedule, you can upgrade the security, execution, and general nature of your site.

Chapter 8: Troubleshooting Common Issues

Diagnosing and Fixing Problems

Diagnosing and fixing issues in WordPress includes a few stages. To begin with, recognize the issue by checking mistake messages, logs, and testing modules/subjects. Then, investigate by deactivating modules, changing to a default subject, and clearing stores. Assuming the issue continues to happen, check for similarity issues, update WordPress, subjects, and modules, and guarantee appropriate record consents. As a last resort, consider reestablishing from reinforcement or looking for help from an engineer or WordPress support discussion.

Also, you can analyze server logs for signs, audit PHP memory restrictions, and incapacitate custom code bits briefly. Check data set trustworthiness utilizing devices like phpMyAdmin, fix ruined tables if important, and upgrade the data set. Routinely reinforce your site to guarantee information security. Use troubleshooting apparatuses like WP_DEBUG to get blunders, and screen server assets for any uncommon spikes. If the issue stays irritating, looking for help from the WordPress people group or recruiting a designer might be prudent for a more top-to-bottom examination.

If you're managing explicit functionalities, assess related code and use program designer apparatuses to distinguish JavaScript or CSS clashes. Run a site well-being check in WordPress for possible issues. For security concerns, reinforce passwords, update security modules, and execute two-factor confirmation. Consistently review client records and eliminate pointless ones. Keep WordPress, subjects, and modules exceptional to fix weaknesses. Finally, consider counseling the WordPress Codex and official discussions for far-reaching investigating guides and local area help.

If you suspect a subject issue, take a stab at reviewing a default topic to check whether the issue continues to happen. Utilize the Wellbeing Check and Investigating module to investigate without influencing your live site. Check for program similarity issues by testing on various programs. Survey server logs and mistake messages for signs on the main driver. Some of the time, a contention between modules can emerge; deliberately deactivate them individually to pinpoint the guilty party.

Make sure to keep reinforcements before rolling out huge improvements, and archive your investigating ventures for future reference. When in doubt, employing an expert WordPress designer or connecting with the authority of WordPress support discussions can give custom-fitted help.

What's more, look at your site's PHP adaptation similarity, guaranteeing it lines up with suggested WordPress necessities. Screen server reaction times and advance server setups. Use instruments like GTmetrix or PageSpeed Experiences to upgrade site execution. Assuming that your site is encountering the "White Screen of Death," check for sentence structure mistakes in your code and increment PHP memory limits.

Consistently review and advance media documents for quicker stacking times. Consider utilizing a Substance Conveyance Organization (CDN) to disseminate content internationally and decrease server load. Executing a storing arrangement, like W3 Complete Reserve or WP Super Reserve, can essentially further develop page load times.

Continuously stay informed about the most recent WordPress best practices and safety efforts to prudently resolve possible issues.

While managing online business issues, guarantee your installment doors and SSL declarations are arranged accurately. Twofold looks at transportation and duty settings to forestall checkout issues. Screen site traffic examples to distinguish and address potential versatility issues.

For Website optimization concerns, use apparatuses like Google Search Control Center to recognize creep mistakes and streamline your webpage structure. Present a refreshed sitemap to web indexes in the wake of making changes. Execute best Website optimization rehearses for content, meta labels, and pictures to improve permeability.

Consistently audit client input and remarks for bits of knowledge into client experience issues. Direct ease-of-use testing to distinguish and address route or configuration concerns. Watch out for portable responsiveness to take special care of a different crowd.

Constant checking, proactive upkeep, and remaining informed about WordPress updates and patterns add to a more vigorous and inconvenience-free site.

If you experience issues with email notices, confirm your email settings inside WordPress and check assuming your facilitating supplier upholds email sending. Introduce and design a dependable SMTP module for more solid email conveyance.

When confronted with login issues, reset passwords, and consider adding extra safety efforts like login endeavor observing or utilizing a security module. Guarantee that client jobs and authorizations are accurately set to control access.

For media-related issues, improve pictures for web utilization and investigate any messed up picture joins. Utilize the media library to oversee documents proficiently, and consider languid stacking pictures for further developed page stacking speed.

Keep in mind that careful documentation of changes made to your site, including updates and arrangements, supports investigating and future upkeep. Consistently investigating your site's exhibition and executing best practices guarantees a smooth WordPress experience.

Chapter 9: Growing Your WordPress Skills

Further Learning Resources

To add to your learning in WordPress, consider investigating web stages like WordPress.org, WPBeginner, and WPMU DEV. Furthermore, look at seminars on stages like Udemy and Coursera, covering points like subject turn of events, module creation, and high-level customization. Taking part in WordPress gatherings and networks can likewise give important experiences and back to your learning process.

Investigate the authority of WordPress Codex for inside and out documentation. Books like "Proficient WordPress" by Brad Williams, David Damstra, and Hal Harsh can offer complete experiences. Go to nearby WordPress meetups or WordCamps for systems administration and active encounters. Follow WordPress specialists on sites and web-based entertainment for the most recent tips and patterns. At last, practice by building your tasks and adding to open-source WordPress modules or subjects on GitHub.

Dig into online instructional exercises on stages like YouTube for visual walkthroughs and pragmatic exhibitions. Consider joining WordPress-zeroed in bunches on LinkedIn or Facebook to associate with experts and fans. Follow WordPress-related web recordings for conversations on industry updates and best practices. Explore different avenues regarding different modules and subjects to acquire involved insight, and routinely look at WordPress people group occasions and online courses for extra learning open doors.

Investigate progressed points like execution streamlining, security, and Website optimization inside the WordPress environment. Get to know coding dialects like PHP, JavaScript, and CSS for more profound customization. Buy into bulletins from legitimate WordPress sites to remain informed about the most recent turns of events. Participate in web-based courses from stages like LinkedIn Learning and Skillshare to improve explicit abilities. Finally, partake in WordPress-related provokes or contests to push your capacities and learn through certifiable tasks.

Consider joining WordPress designer networks on stages like GitHub to team up on projects and gain from others' code. Follow WordPress-related hashtags on Twitter to remain refreshed on conversations and industry news. Investigate WordPress-related digital recordings like "WP Bar" or "Matt Report" for bits of knowledge from specialists. Take part in discussions like Stack Trade WordPress to seek clarification on pressing issues and offer information. Routinely look at the WordPress official blog for declarations and updates. Also, remember to investigate particular discussions for explicit viewpoints like WooCommerce or Gutenberg assuming you're working with those elements.

Joining WordPress Communities

Joining a WordPress people group is an extraordinary method for interfacing with different devotees, sharing information, and remaining refreshed. Consider stages like WordPress discussions, nearby meetups, or online gatherings to draw in individual clients and engineers.

Investigate WordPress.org gatherings for investigating and conversations, go to neighborhood WordPress meetups or WordCamps for in-person systems administration and join online networks on stages like Leeway or Dissension. Drawing in with these networks can give important bits of knowledge, backing, and amazing chances to team up with others in the WordPress environment.

Moreover, adding to the WordPress Center, subjects, or modules on stages like GitHub is a brilliant approach to effectively take an interest and improve your abilities while being important for the more extensive WordPress people group. Remain refreshed on WordPress-related writes and digital broadcasts for industry bits of knowledge and patterns.

You can likewise partake in WordPress-related virtual entertainment bunches on stages like LinkedIn or Facebook, where you can share your mastery, clarify some pressing issues, and associate with experts in the field. Consider joining particular gatherings or gatherings in light of your particular advantages inside the WordPress environment for additional designated conversations.

Besides, going to virtual meetings or online classes committed to WordPress can extend your insight and furnish chances to collaborate with specialists. Take part in discussions on Twitter utilizing significant hashtags to associate with the WordPress people group and remain informed about the most recent turns of events and conversations.

Investigate WordPress-related digital recordings for adroit conversations and meetings with industry specialists. Effectively partaking in discussions on stages like Stack Trade can likewise offer an alternate point of view and assist you with gaining from different encounters inside the WordPress people group.

Consider joining WordPress-centered email bulletins to get normal updates, tips, and arranged content straightforwardly in your inbox. Teaming up on open-source undertakings or offering help to others locally can lay out a positive presence and fabricate significant associations inside the WordPress biological system.

Moreover, joining particular LinkedIn bunches connected with WordPress improvement, plan, or explicit specialties can give a stage to proficient systems administration and information trade. Remember to share your encounters and bits of knowledge, adding to the aggregate mastery of the WordPress people group.

Exploring Advanced Features

WordPress offers a scope of cutting edge elements to upgrade your site. This incorporates custom post types, scientific classifications, and custom fields for content association. Furthermore, you can execute progressed Web optimization techniques with modules like Yoast Search engine optimization. Investigate subjects with worked in customization choices, use page developers like Elementor for a unique plan, and consider coordinating web based business usefulness utilizing modules like WooCommerce. Remember about security - carry areas of strength for out, normal reinforcements, and security modules like Wordfence.

Dive into WordPress multisite for dealing with numerous destinations from a solitary establishment. Utilize the REST Programming interface to associate and communicate with outer applications. Execute client jobs and authorizations for exact command over happy supporters. Investigate reserving modules like W3 Complete Store for further developed site speed. Influence custom snares and channels for cutting edge subject and module customization. Stay up to date with the most recent Gutenberg manager highlights for improved content creation. In conclusion, consider involving outsider administrations for examination, and email promoting, and that's just the beginning, coordinating them consistently into your WordPress site.

Exploit WordPress CLI (Order Line Connection point) for productive site the board through the order line. Execute a responsive plan for ideal client experience across different gadgets. Investigate A/B testing utilizing modules like Nelio or Google Enhance to streamline your site's exhibition. Use CDN (Content Conveyance Organization) administrations to improve stacking speeds around the world. Jump into the universe of podcasting or video content by coordinating particular modules. In conclusion, hold your site's exhibition under control with devices like Question Screen for troubleshooting and observing.

Consider carrying out a participation framework utilizing modules like MemberPress or Limit Content Expert for elite substance access. Improve client commitment with web-based entertainment combinations utilizing modules like Social Fighting or Shared Counts. Explore different avenues regarding dynamic substance through restrictive rationale modules like Assuming this is the case or Dynamic Circumstances. For cutting edge customizations, investigate making your own custom modules or subjects customized to your particular requirements. Remain refreshed on the most recent WordPress patterns and updates to exploit new highlights and upgrades consistently added to the stage.

Upgrade your site's exhibition by compacting pictures with modules like Smush or ShortPixel. Execute languid stacking to further develop page stacking times, particularly for picture weighty locales. Investigate the utilization of custom gadgets and sidebars for exceptional substance designs. Consider carrying out an organizing climate utilizing modules like WP Arranging for testing refreshes prior to applying them to your live site. Use Google Examination or other investigation devices for inside and out bits of knowledge into your site's traffic and client conduct. In conclusion, remain informed about availability guidelines and guarantee your site is open to clients with handicaps by utilizing modules like WP Availability.

Chapter 10: Conclusion

Recap and Next Steps

To recap, WordPress is a well-known content administration framework (CMS) used to make and oversee sites. It offers adaptability, convenience, and an extensive variety of modules and topics for customization.

For the following stages, consider:

Content Creation: Begin adding pages and presents on your site.

Customization: Investigate subjects and modules to tailor your site's appearance and usefulness.

Website optimization: Enhance your substance for web search tools to further develop permeability.

Security: Execute safety efforts, such as solid passwords and standard reinforcements.

Refreshes: Keep WordPress, subjects, and modules state-of-the-art for ideal execution and security.

Here are extra subsequent stages for improving your WordPress site:

Portable Improvement: Guarantee your site is dynamic for a consistent client experience on cell phones and tablets.

Execution Streamlining: Accelerate your site by enhancing pictures, utilizing storing modules, and picking a dependable facilitating supplier.

Client Commitment: Support collaboration through remarks, social sharing, and perhaps coordinating discussions or local area highlights.

Investigation: Set up instruments like Google Examination to follow guest conduct, assisting you with grasping your crowd and working on happiness.

Adaptation: If relevant, investigate choices for adapting your site, for example, offshoot showcasing, promotions, or selling items/administrations.

Pamphlet: Execute a bulletin information exchange to construct a mailing rundown and keep guests refreshed on new happiness or contributions.

Availability: Guarantee your site is open to all clients, incorporating those with inabilities, by following accepted procedures.

Keep in mind, that steady upgrades and normal support add to an effective WordPress site.

The following are a couple of additional moves toward upgrading your WordPress experience:

Web-based Entertainment Mix: Associate your website with online entertainment stages to build permeability and offer substance without any problem.

Reinforcement Procedure: Execute a dependable reinforcement framework to shield your site information. Consistently reinforce the two records and the information base.

Multilingual Help: On the off chance that your crowd is different, consider adding multilingual help to make your substance open to a more extensive crowd.

SSL Authentication: Guarantee your site has an SSL declaration for secure information transmission, and it can decidedly affect your web index positioning.

404 Page Customization: Make a tweaked 404 blunder page to direct guests back to your substance on the off chance that they experience a wrecked connection.

Lawful Consistence: Check and guarantee that your site conforms to legitimate prerequisites, like protection arrangements, terms of administration, and treatment.

Execution Observing: Use devices like PageSpeed Bits of Knowledge to screen your site's exhibition and address any issues influencing stacking times.

Client Preparing: If others will deal with the site, give preparation on fundamental WordPress works and best practices to keep up with consistency.

Here are extra moves toward improving your WordPress site:

Construction Markup: Carry out mapping markup to give web search tools additional background information about your substance, possibly further developing indexed lists.

Custom Post Types: Investigate making custom post types for explicit substance, taking into account better association and showing on your site.

Enhance Permalinks: Use Web optimization agreeable permalinks for your posts and pages. Redo them to be distinct and incorporate pertinent watchwords.

Picture Pressure: Streamline pictures for the web by compacting them without compromising quality. This assists with quicker stacking times.

Remark Balance: Set up remark control to sift through spam and guarantee a positive client experience in the remark segment.

Content Schedule: Plan your substance ahead of time by making a substance schedule. This can assist with keeping up with consistency and draw in your crowd routinely.

Organizing Climate: Consider involving an arranging climate for testing changes before applying them to your live site, limiting the gamble of mistakes.

WordPress Security Modules: Introduce legitimate security modules to add a layer of insurance against expected dangers and weaknesses.

Broken Connection Checker: Consistently check for broken joins on your site and fix them to further develop client experience and keep up with Website design enhancement.

Draw in with Local area: Join WordPress discussions, and networks, or go to neighborhood meetups to remain refreshed on the most recent patterns and get support from the local area.

These means cover a scope of viewpoints to guarantee your WordPress site is very much upgraded, secure, and locked in.

Embracing Your WordPress Journey

Setting out on your WordPress venture opens ways to vast opportunities for site creation and customization. Remain inquisitive, investigate different subjects and modules, and make it a point for local area support when required. Blissful WordPress!

As you dive further into WordPress, center around refining your plan abilities, advancing site execution, and dominating Web optimization methods. Routinely update your insight with the developing WordPress environment to take full advantage of its dynamic highlights. Partake in the educational experience and praise your achievements en route!

Consider joining discussions and going to WordPress meetups to interface with individual devotees, trade bits of knowledge, and investigate difficulties. Embrace the iterative idea of site advancement, constantly refining and adjusting your substance in light of client criticism and examination. Keep in mind, your WordPress venture is an imaginative experience, so enjoy the most common way of rejuvenating your novel thoughts on the web.

www.ingramcontent.com/pod-product-compliance
Lightning Source LLC
Chambersburg PA
CBHW012305240726
48656CB00008B/2551